CHRISTMAS COOKIES

to make and bake

CHRISTMAS COOKIES

to make and bake

25 DELICIOUSLY FUN RECIPES

RYLAND PETERS & SMALL
LONDON • NEW YORK

NOTES

- Both British (Metric) plus American (Imperial plus US cups as appropriate) are included in these recipes for your convenience; however it is important to work with one set of measurements and not alternate between the two within a recipe.

- When a prepared baking sheet is called for in the recipes, this means one that has been lightly greased with butter and lined with non-stick baking parchment trimmed to fit.

- All spoon measurements are level unless otherwise specified.

- All eggs are large (UK) which is extra-large (US). Uncooked or partially cooked eggs should not be served to the very old, frail, young children, pregnant women or those with compromised immune systems. Please note that the recipe for Royal Icing given on page 8 contains uncooked egg whites.

- Ovens should be preheated to the specified temperatures. We recommend using an oven thermometer. If using a fan-assisted oven, adjust temperatures according to the manufacturer's instructions.

- Always store baked cookies (once they are cool) in airtight containers in a cool and dry place and store like with like to avoid flavour contamination or changes in texture.

Designers Paul Stradling and Eoghan O'Brien

Production Controller Mai-Ling Collyer

Editorial Director Julia Charles

Publisher Cindy Richards

Indexer Hilary Bird

First published in 2015
This edition published in 2016 by
Ryland Peters & Small
20–21 Jockey's Fields
London WC1R 4BW
and
Ryland Peters & Small Inc.
341 E 116th St
New York NY 10029

www.rylandpeters.com

Text © Annie Rigg, Catherine Woram, Chloe Coker, Gerhard Jenne, Hannah Miles, Isidora Popovic, Julian Day, Laura Tabor, Liz Franklin, Mickael Benichou, Sarah Randell, Tessa Evelegh and Ryland Peters & Small 2015, 2016

Design and photographs
© Ryland Peters & Small 2015, 2016

ISBN: 978-1-84975-643-3

10 9 8 7 6 5 4 3 2

A CIP record for this book is available from the British Library.

US Library of Congress Cataloging-in-Publication data has been applied for.

Printed and bound in China

CONTENTS

INTRODUCTION

Cookies are made for sharing and what could be more festive than baking delicious treats that will fill your home with the warming, spiced smells of Christmas?

At this special time of year, everything takes on a magical sparkle and feels that little bit more special, and baking is no exception. Giving and receiving are such an important part of the Christmas tradition and home-baked cookies and other sweet treats packaged in cellophane bags or boxes and tied with ribbons are guaranteed to bring a smile to the faces of all those lucky enough to receive them, whether it's much-loved grandparents, thoughtful neighbours or a favourite teacher.

There is something here for everyone, so whether you are a novice baker or an expert, there is no excuse not to put on your best apron, reach for the icing sugar duster and sparkly sprinkles and create some unique magical Christmas memories in the warmth of your own kitchen.

ICING TECHNIQUES

The recipes in this book mostly use two types of icings and both are available in the baking aisle of supermarkets. Ready-to-roll fondant icing can be found in a variety of colours and is used to cut into shapes and applied to cookies. Royal icing is used for piping and flooding (see opposite) and can be made using shop-bought Royal Icing Sugar (simply following the instructions given on the pack), or see below for how to make the Royal Icing from scratch.

ROYAL ICING

2 very fresh egg whites
500–600 g/4½ cups icing/
   confectioners' sugar, sifted

Place the ingredients in the bowl of a stand mixer fitted with a paddle attachment and beat for 5–7 minutes, until white and thick. Alternatively use a mixing bowl and hand-held electric whisk. Beat the egg whites until foamy and whisk in the sugar. For piping it should hold a solid ribbon trail. If you are not using it immediately, cover with clingfilm/plastic wrap, pressing it into the surface to prevent the icing from drying out. Refrigerate until needed (see note on page 4).

USING ROYAL ICING

TINTING ICING

Divide the icing into separate bowls. It's best to use food colouring pastes for tinting royal icing. This is available in small pots and in a vast array of colours. A tiny amount of colouring goes a long way, so use it with caution. Use a cocktail stick/toothpick to gradually add dots of colouring to the icing and mix well before adding more colour until you achieve the desired shade.

OUTLINING

You will need piping bags to create the outlines and details on each cookie. You can buy clear plastic disposable bags from good kitchenware shops, sugarcraft specialists and online suppliers (as shown in the photos, right); or make your own from greaseproof paper, folded into a cone, with the tip snipped off. When outlining, pipe as close to the edge of the cookie as possible. Hold the bag at a 45-degree angle, apply even pressure (squeezing from the top of the bag, not the middle), and move the bag steadily along the cookie. Leave the outline to dry for a few minutes before flooding the cookie.

FLOODING

For flooding you will need to thin the icing with a little water until it reaches the consistency of emulsion paint. Add water a teaspoonful at a time until you get the right consistency. Spread some icing onto the cookie, keeping it away from the edges. Spread enough icing onto the cookie so that it looks generously covered, but not so much that it overflows. Use a round-bladed knife to guide the icing so that it floods any gaps. Once you have flooded the cookie, check the surface for any air bubbles and pop them with a cocktail stick/toothpick. Leave the icing to set completely before applying any further decoration.

DECORATIONS

These pretty festive ornaments are made using a versatile basic spiced gingerbread dough. If you want to thread them with ribbon and hang them from the Christmas tree, remember to make a hole in the top before baking.

CHRISTMAS BAUBLES

Beat together the golden syrup and egg yolk in a small bowl. Sift the flour, baking powder, spices and salt into a mixing bowl and add the butter. Rub the butter into the flour mixture with your fingertips. When the mixture starts to look like sand, add the sugar and mix in with your fingers to incorporate. Add the egg-yolk mixture and mix with a wooden spoon until starting to clump together. Tip the mixture out onto a very lightly floured surface and knead gently to bring together into a smooth ball. Flatten the dough into a disc, wrap in clingfilm/plastic wrap and refrigerate for 1–2 hours.

Preheat the oven to 170°C (325°F) Gas 3. Lightly dust a clean, dry surface with flour and roll the dough evenly to a thickness of 2–3 mm/⅛ inch. Use the cutters to stamp out as many cookies as possible from the dough. Arrange the cookies on the prepared baking sheets. Gather the dough scraps together, knead lightly, re-roll and stamp out more cookies until all the dough has been used up. Use a cocktail stick/toothpick to make a hole in the top of each cookie if you plan to hang them. Bake the baubles in batches on the middle shelf of the preheated oven for 10–12 minutes or until firm and lightly browned at the edges. Allow the cookies to cool completely on the baking sheets before icing.

Prepare the Royal Icing. Transfer half the icing to another bowl and tint using the pink food colouring paste (see page 9 for help with Tinting). Tint the other half violet. Fill a disposable piping bag with 3 tablespoons of the pink icing. Take some of the cookies and pipe outlines around each one. (See page 9 for help with Outlining and Flooding.) Add more pink colouring paste to the remaining pink icing to make a deeper shade, if you like, and pipe outlines around more cookies. Take another piping bag and spoon 3 tablespoons of the violet icing into it. Pipe an outline around the remaining cookies with the violet icing. Allow the icing to set for 10 minutes. Flood the insides of the outlines with a corresponding or contrasting colour. Allow to dry for 20 minutes. Pipe decorative patterns in contrasting colours on each ornament and decorate with edible balls and glitter. Allow the icing to set completely before threading with fine ribbon, if using.

BASIC SPICED GINGERBREAD

- 2 tablespoons golden/corn syrup
- 1 egg yolk
- 200 g/1⅔ cups plain/all-purpose flour, plus extra for dusting
- ½ teaspoon baking powder
- 1½ teaspoons ground ginger
- 1 teaspoon ground cinnamon
- ¼ teaspoon freshly grated nutmeg
- a pinch of salt
- 100 g/7 tablespoons unsalted butter, chilled and diced
- 75 g/⅓ cup light muscovado or light brown soft sugar

TO DECORATE

- 1 quantity Royal Icing (see page 8)
- pink and violet food colouring pastes
- edible metallic balls and edible glitter

Christmas ornament-shaped cutters in assorted designs and sizes
2 prepared baking sheets
disposable piping bags

MAKES 12–16

SUPER-SIMPLE TREE DECORATIONS

75 g/6 tablespoons unsalted butter, softened

115 g/½ cup caster/granulated sugar

1 egg

200 g/1½ cups plain/all-purpose flour

½ teaspoon baking powder

½ teaspoon salt

TO DECORATE

tubes of ready-made icing in a variety of colours

cookie cutters in assorted shapes

plastic drinking straw

1 prepared baking sheet

ribbon or ric rac braid

MAKES 18

Preheat the oven to 180°C (350°F) Gas 4. Cream the butter and sugar until soft, and then beat in the egg. Sift in the flour, baking powder and salt. Roll the dough into a ball, wrap in clingfilm/plastic wrap, and put in the fridge for about 1 hour.

Roll out the cookie mixture to a thickness of approximately 1 cm/ ½ inch and use the cookie cutters to cut out the different shapes. Arrange the shapes on the prepared baking sheet. Cut the straw to a length of about 10 cm/4 inches using scissors and pierce the top of each cookie with it to make a good-size hole for the ribbon.

Bake the cookies in the preheated oven for about 8–10 minutes or until golden brown. Remove the cookies from the oven and place them on a wire rack. Use the straw to repierce the holes if they have closed up during cooking. Leave the cookies to cool before decorating each one with the ready-made icing.

Cut pieces of ribbon or ric rac braid and thread them through the holes in each cookie to finish.

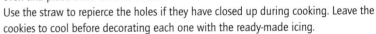

These sweet little cookies are perfect to make with the children. A basic sugar dough is stamped out in simple shapes and decorated using ready-made coloured icing in squeezy tubes which means it's easy for small hands to use and makes less mess! Bake the cookies and once they are cool let the little ones express themselves!

These intricate snowflake cookies with their jewel-like effect in a rainbow of festive colours look beautiful hung in a window to catch the light and make the perfect edible Christmas decoration.

STAINED GLASS COOKIES

BASIC VANILLA COOKIE DOUGH
225 g/1 stick plus 7 tablespoons
   unsalted butter, softened

225 g/1 cup plus 2 tablespoons
   caster/granulated sugar

1 egg, beaten

½ teaspoon vanilla extract

a pinch of salt

450 g/3½ cups plain/all-purpose
   flour, sifted, plus extra for dusting

TO DECORATE
1 bag fruit-flavoured boiled
   sweets/hard candies

2 prepared baking sheets

snowflake cookie cutters in assorted sizes

metallic thread

MAKES 24

Cream together the butter and sugar until light and creamy. Add the beaten egg, vanilla and salt and mix well. Gradually add the flour and mix until incorporated. Bring together into a dough, then flatten into a disc. Wrap in clingfilm/plastic wrap and refrigerate for 2 hours.

Roll the dough out on a lightly floured work surface to a thickness of about 3–4 mm/¼ inch. Using the cookie cutters, stamp out shapes. Arrange them on the prepared baking sheets. Gather together the off-cuts of the dough and re-roll to make more shapes. Use a cocktail stick/toothpick to make a hole in the top of each cookie. Refrigerate on the baking sheets for 15 minutes. Preheat the oven to 180°C (350°F) Gas 4.

Divide the boiled sweets/hard candies into separate colours and pop into plastic food bags. Using a rolling pin, crush them into small pieces. Take the baking sheets of cookies out of the fridge. Carefully fill the empty spaces in the snowflake-shapes with the crushed sweets in an even, thin layer and no thicker than the depth of the cookies. Bake one sheet at a time on the middle shelf of the preheated oven for about 12 minutes, or until the cookies are pale

golden and the sweets/candies have melted to fill the spaces and create a beautiful stained-glass effect. Leave the cookies to cool completely on the baking sheets until the 'stained glass' has set. Thread some metallic thread through the holes to finish.

ADVENT SHORTBREAD

To make the vanilla shortbread, beat the butter in a mixing bowl with a wooden spoon until smooth and very soft. Meanwhile, sift together the flour and salt. Add the icing/confectioners' sugar to the creamed butter and continue mixing until light and fluffy. Add the vanilla and mix again. Add the sifted flour and salt and mix until it starts to come together into a dough.

To knead the dough, first sprinkle a little flour on a clean work surface. Then shape the dough into a ball and push on it and press it onto the work surface, turning it round often. Do this for a minute, then flatten into a disc, cover with clingfilm/plastic wrap and chill until needed.

To make the chocolate shortbread, follow the steps above, but add the cocoa powder to the flour and salt.

Preheat the oven to 180°C (350°F) Gas 4.

Sprinkle more flour on the work surface. Using a rolling pin, roll out the vanilla and chocolate dough (separately) to a thickness of 2–3 mm/⅛ inch and stamp out 24 shapes using the assorted cookie cutters. Arrange on the prepared baking sheets. Using the numbered cutters, stamp out numbers 1–24 and stick to each larger cookie with a dab of cold water. Leave the cookies to chill in the fridge for about 10 minutes.

Put one baking sheet on the middle shelf of the preheated oven. Bake for about 12 minutes, or until firm and starting to go crisp at the edges. Repeat with the second batch of cookies.

Remove the cookies from the oven and leave to cool on the baking sheets before packaging into cellophane bags, into which holes have been punched and ribbon threaded.

VANILLA SHORTBREAD

225 g/1 stick plus 7 tablespoons unsalted butter, softened

250 g/2 cups plain/all-purpose flour

½ teaspoon salt

75 g/½ cup icing/confectioners' sugar, sifted

1 teaspoon vanilla extract

CHOCOLATE SHORTBREAD

225 g/1 stick plus 7 tablespoons unsalted butter, softened

200 g/1⅔ cups plain/all-purpose flour

50 g/⅓ cup cocoa powder

½ teaspoon salt

75 g/½ cup icing/confectioners' sugar, sifted

1 teaspoon vanilla extract

cookie cutters in assorted shapes

numbered cookie cutters

1–2 prepared baking sheets

24 cellophane bags and ribbon

MAKES 24

You will need a selection of numbered cookie cutters,
preferably in different sizes, and plain cutters in
different shapes to make these. Give them away
to friends and family to celebrate Advent.

These decorated cookies are a rich gingerbread baked with dark treacle and a hint of cocoa. Thread festive ribbons through them so that they can be tied around napkins at the Christmas table.

JOLLY HOLLY WREATHS

Beat together the golden/corn syrup, treacle/molasses and egg yolk in a small bowl. Sift the flour, baking powder, cocoa, spices and salt into a food processor (or into a mixing bowl) and add the butter. When the mixture starts to look like sand and there are no lumps of butter, add the sugar and almonds and pulse (or mix with your fingers) again for 30 seconds to incorporate. With the motor running, add the egg-yolk mixture and pulse (or mix with a wooden spoon) until starting to clump together. Tip the mixture out onto a lightly floured surface and knead gently to bring together into a smooth ball. Flatten into a disc, wrap in clingfilm/plastic wrap and chill for 1–2 hours. Preheat the oven to 170°C (325°F) Gas 3.

Lightly dust a clean, dry surface with flour and roll the dough evenly to a thickness of 2–3 mm/⅛ inch. Using the larger cookie cutter, stamp out discs and arrange on the prepared baking sheets, spacing the cookies apart. Use the smaller cutter to stamp out discs from the middle of each cookie. Gather the dough scraps together, knead lightly, re-roll and stamp out more cookies until all the dough has been used up. Bake the gingerbread in batches on the middle shelf of the preheated oven for 10–12 minutes or until firm and browned at the edges. Allow the cookies to cool completely on the baking sheets before icing.

Prepare the Royal Icing. Divide the icing between 3 bowls. Tint 2 of the bowls different shades of green (see page 9 for help with Tinting). Thicken each one by beating it vigorously for a minute or by adding more icing/confectioners' sugar. Leave the remaining bowl of icing white. Fill a disposable piping bag with about 4 teaspoons of one green icing and pipe an outline around the outside and inside edges of each cookie. (See page 9 for help with Outlining.) Allow to dry for at least 10 minutes. Flood the outlines with white icing (see page 9 for help with Flooding). Allow to dry for 20 minutes.

Fit a piping bag with the leaf nozzle and fill with one shade of green icing. Pipe leaf shapes over the white icing. Repeat with the other shade of green icing until you have full, leafy wreaths. Dust with edible glitter. Tint the remaining white icing red, spoon into another piping bag and pipe small holly berries among the leaves. Allow the icing to set completely before threading with ribbon.

CHOCOLATE GINGERBREAD

2 tablespoons golden/corn syrup

2 tablespoons dark treacle/molasses

1 egg yolk

200 g/1⅔ cups plain/all-purpose flour, plus extra for rolling out

1 teaspoon baking powder

25 g/3 tablespoons cocoa powder

2 teaspoons ground ginger

½ teaspoon ground cinnamon

a pinch of salt

75 g/5 tablespoons unsalted butter, chilled and diced

75 g/⅓ cup dark brown soft sugar

50 g/½ cup ground almonds

TO DECORATE

Royal Icing (see page 8)

green and red food colouring pastes

edible green glitter

2 round fluted cookie cutters, 8 cm/3 inch and 3 cm/1 inch

prepared baking sheets

disposable piping bags

small leaf-shaped piping nozzle/tip

MAKES 12–14

SPARKLY SNOWFLAKES

SPICED GINGER COOKIES

375 g/scant 3 cups plain/all-purpose flour, plus extra for dusting

½ teaspoon baking powder

1 teaspoon bicarbonate of/baking soda

1 teaspoon ground cinnamon

3 teaspoons ground ginger

¼ each teaspoon ground cloves, nutmeg and allspice

a pinch of salt

125 g/1 stick unsalted butter, softened

75 g/⅓ cup light brown soft sugar

1 egg beaten

3 tablespoons clear honey

3 tablespoons black treacle/molasses

1 tablespoon lemon juice

TO DECORATE

icing sugar/confectioners' sugar, for rolling out

300 g/10 oz. white ready-to-roll fondant icing

2 tablespoons apricot jam, warmed

½ quantity Royal Icing (see page 8)

white edible glitter and nonpareils

snowflake cookie cutters in assorted designs and sizes

2 prepared baking sheets

small piping bag with a fine nozzle

embossing tools (optional)

MAKES 12–16

Sift together the flour, baking powder, bicarbonate of/baking soda, spices and salt. Cream together the butter and sugar until light and creamy. Add the beaten egg, honey, molasses and lemon juice and mix until smooth. Add the sifted dry ingredients and mix again until smooth. Knead the dough lightly, just enough to bring it together, then wrap in clingfilm/plastic wrap and refrigerate for 2 hours.

Preheat the oven to 180°C (350°F) Gas 4. Take the dough out of the fridge and put it on a lightly floured work surface. Roll it out to a thickness of 3–4 mm/¼ inch. Using the snowflake cookie cutters, stamp out shapes and arrange them on the prepared baking sheets. Gather together the off-cuts of the dough and re-roll to make more shapes. Use a cocktail stick/toothpick to make a hole in the top of each cookie if you plan to hang them.

Bake the cookies on the middle shelf of the preheated oven for 10–12 minutes, or until firm and the edges are just starting to brown. Leave to cool on the sheets for about 5 minutes before transferring to a wire rack to cool completely.

Lightly dust a work surface with icing/confectioners' sugar. Roll out the fondant icing to a thickness of 3 mm/⅛ inch. Using the cookie cutters, stamp out snowflakes to match each of your cookies. Lightly brush the top of each cold cookie with the warmed apricot jam. Position one fondant snowflake on top of each cookie, gently smoothing it into place with your hands. Fill the piping bag with the Royal Icing and pipe a border of lines or dots around the edge of the fondant icing on each cookie. While the royal icing is still wet, sprinkle edible glitter, lustres and nonpareils over it so that they stick in place.

Using embossing tools, press decorative patterns into the fondant icing. If you have through the fondant to make a hole in the same place. Leave the cookies to dry, then push a length of thread through each hole and tie a knot to secure.

Look out for snowflake cookie cutters in sets of assorted shapes and sizes. Once covered in fondant icing, these cookies can be decorated in a vast array of nonpareils, lustres and glitters, which all help to create a frosted and sparkly winter wonderland feel.

CHRISTMAS TREE STACK

Preheat the oven to 180°C (350°F) Gas 4.

Put the butter, sugar and flour in a large mixing bowl. Rub together until the mixture resembles fine breadcrumbs, and then add the egg yolk. Bring everything together to form a smooth dough.

On a clean, lightly floured work surface, roll out the dough into a large rectangle about 4 mm/¼ in. thick. Cut out star shapes in descending sizes. Bring the trimmed dough together and roll out again to cut as many cookies out of the dough as possible. Arrange the cookies on the prepared baking sheets, with the larger cookies on one sheet and the smaller cookies on another.

Bake the larger cookies in the preheated oven for 8–10 minutes, and the smaller for 4–8 minutes, until golden and firm. Leave to cool on the baking sheets for 10 minutes or so, before transferring to a wire rack until completely cold.

Roll out the fondant icing and cut into stars using the cookie cutters, so that you have fondant stars that correspond in size to the cookies. Brush the cold cookies with the melted apricot jam and position the matching fondant star on top. Push gently to secure, taking care not to break the cookies.

Tint the Royal Icing green (see page 9 for help with Tinting) and spoon it into the piping bag. Outline the cookies with a green line (see page 9 for help with Outlining). Decorate the edges of each star with silver balls, gently pushing them into the piped green icing to secure.

When the icing is dry stack the cookies on a serving plate, starting with the largest cookie at the base, as positioning as shown. Scatter over some loose nonpareils and sprinkles to finish.

120 g/1 stick butter
120 g/²⁄₃ cup caster/granulated sugar
180 g/1 ⅓ cups plain/all-purpose flour
1 egg, separated

TO DECORATE
500 g/16 oz. green ready-to-roll fondant icing
50 g/¼ cup apricot jam, melted
½ quantity of Royal Icing (see page 8)
green food colouring paste
edible silver balls, nonpareils and other sprinkles of your choice

star-shaped cookie cutters in various sizes
2 prepared baking sheets
a disposable piping bag

MAKES 1

A lovely stack of crisp, buttery cookies, made to look like an elegant Christmas tree is a very special thing to make for Christmas. You can buy individual star cookie cutters in descending sizes, or search out the kits that are especially made for the purpose. These usually include about 10 cookie cutters from very large for the base, to very tiny ones for the top.

These cute cookies were inspired by
a vintage Christmas card and are a
kitsch take on the traditional English
Christmas pudding. Make them
with gingerbread dough or chocolate
gingerbread for some Chrismas spice.

CHRISTMAS PUDDINGS

1 recipe Basic Spiced Gingerbread
(see page 11) or Chocolate
Gingerbread (see page 19)

TO DECORATE
icing/confectioners sugar, for dusting
125 g/4oz each white, red, blue, green
ready-to-roll fondant icing
2 tablespoons apricot jam, warmed

a round 7-cm/3-inch cookie cutter
holly-leaf plunger cutter
mini round cutters

MAKES 12

Prepare and bake your cookies following the method on page 11 or 19 as appropriate and using the cookie cutter specified here. Allow them to cool completely before you begin decorating them.

Dust the work surface with icing/confectioners' sugar and roll out the red, blue and green rolled fondant to a thickness of 3 mm/⅛ inch. Roll small balls of white fondant and squash them onto the 3 different-coloured rolled fondants with your thumb. Gently roll over the rolled fondant again with a rolling pin to create a polka dot effect. Using the same cookie cutter that you used for the cookies, cut out 4 rounds from each colour from the rolled fondant and attach them to the cookies following the method for covering cookies given on page 20. Next cut out 6 circles of white rolled fondant and using a small sharp knife, cut a wavy line through each circle to create 12 half circles. Take each half circle and attach it to each covered cookie as before.

Decorate the puddings as you wish. You can make buttons using the mini round cutters (using a cocktail stick/toothpick to create holes and score the edges), use a plunger cutter to make holly leaves, make roses by rolling a thin sausage of rolled fondant and squashing it with your thumb, or simple bows by cutting out 2 strips of fondant about 1 cm/½ inch wide and folding them to create a bow and ribbon tails in 2 separate pieces as shown above. Leave to dry for 1 hour before serving.

SNOWMAN COOKIES

Put the flour, butter, sugar, egg, golden/corn syrup and cinnamon, if using, in the bowl of an electric stand mixer and beat together until combined. Bring the dough together with your hands, then wrap in clingfilm/plastic wrap and refrigerate for 1 hour or longer.

Preheat the oven to 180°C (350°F) Gas 4.

Tip half the dough out onto a lightly floured work surface and roll out until it is 4–5 mm/¼ inch thick. Using the cutter, stamp out 12 rounds and arrange them on the baking sheets. Bake in the preheated oven for 10–12 minutes, or until lightly golden. Leave to cool on wire racks.

Repeat with the other half of the dough.

To decorate, lightly dust the work surface and a rolling pin with icing/confectioners' sugar. Roll out half the white icing until it is 3 mm/⅛ inch thick. Using the cutter again, stamp out 12 rounds. Repeat with the other half of the icing.

Put a dab of golden syrup in the centre of each cookie to act as glue and place a round of white icing on each one. Make 2 eyes on each snowman by pressing 2 currant halves into the icing quite firmly.

Next, using your hands, roll 24 small, carrot-shaped noses from the orange icing, making indentations along the length of each one with a small knife. Stick the noses onto the snowman faces with the tiniest dab of water.

Roll the red icing into 24 short, thin strips and pinch the ends. Stick one to each face for a mouth.

Using a rolling pin again, roll out the black, blue or green icing, in batches, and cut out hat shapes. Make indentations for the brims. Stick the hats on, then leave the snowmen to dry for an hour or so before serving.

225 g/1¾ cups self-raising/rising flour, sifted

100 g/6½ tablespoons unsalted butter, softened

100 g/½ cup light brown soft sugar

1 egg

1 tablespoon golden/corn syrup

a pinch of ground cinnamon

TO DECORATE
icing/confectioners' sugar, for dusting

400 g/14 oz. white ready-to-roll fondant icing

2 teaspoons golden/corn syrup

24 currants, halved

about 50 g/2 oz. orange ready-to-roll fondant icing

about 50 g/2 oz. red ready-to-roll fondant icing

150 g/6 oz. black, blue or green ready-to-roll fondant icing

a round 7-cm/3-inch cookie cutter

2 prepared baking sheets

MAKES 24

These are fun to make with children. If you don't want to have to buy three types of coloured icing, use red for both the noses and the mouths — or tiny pieces of candied peel also make fine snowman noses.

1 quantity Spiced Ginger Cookie dough
(see page 20)

TO DECORATE
plain/all-purpose flour, for dusting

2 quantities Royal Icing (see page 8)

red food colouring paste

black food colouring paste

red, pink and white heart- and star-
shaped sugar sprinkles

Russian doll-shaped paper templates
(see note on opposite page)

2 prepared baking sheets

small piping bag fitted with a fine
writing nozzle

mini palette knife or small knife

MAKES ABOUT 8–10 DEPENDING ON SIZE

RUSSIAN DOLLS

Roll out the Spiced Ginger Cookie dough to a thickness of 3–4 mm/¼ inch on a lightly floured work surface. Lay your paper templates directly on top of the dough and cut around using a small, sharp knife. Arrange them on the prepared baking sheets. Gather together the off-cuts of the dough and re-roll to make more shapes. Refrigerate for 15 minutes.

Preheat the oven to 180°C (350°F) Gas 4.

Bake the cookies on the middle shelf of the preheated oven for about 12 minutes, or until firm, swapping the sheets over if needed. Leave to cool on the baking sheets for about 10 minutes before transferring to a wire rack to cool completely.

Divide the Royal Icing between 3 bowls. Tint one red and one black (see page 9 for help on Tinting) using the food colouring pastes. Leave the third bowl of icing white.

Fill the piping bag with whichever colour you want to start with. Pipe borders around the cold cookies. If you want to make the 'belly' of the doll in the other colour of icing, you will need to create a border for this too. Flood the area inside the borders with icing (see page 9 for help on Flooding). Once you have made a neat border, you can spoon icing within the borders and spread it carefully up to the edges with a mini palette knife or small knife. Leave to dry and harden slightly before going any further.

Pipe in the rest of the design and the dolls' faces. Now pipe small flowers, dots, squiggles and whatever you like over the dolls and add heart and star-shaped sugar sprinkles to embellish your designs. Leave to dry for an hour or so before serving.

Look out for images of Russian dolls on wrapping paper or cards and use them as templates for these cookies. If you find a shape you like you can photocopy it in 3 different sizes. Then simply cut out the paper template, lay it onto the rolled-out cookie dough and cut around it using a small, sharp knife.

Everyone loves gingerbread men — both making them and eating them! These simple shapes are great fun to decorate and the classic cutters are widely available in all shapes and sizes. Here they are iced very simply, but feel free to give this family whatever clothes you like. Using sugar-coated chocolate drops for buttons adds some colour but the more traditional decoration would be raisins.

GINGERBREAD FAMILY

Prepare the Basic Spiced Gingerbread dough according to the recipe on page 11. Preheat the oven to 170°C (325°F) Gas 3.

Lightly dust a clean, dry surface with flour and roll the dough evenly to a thickness of 2–3 mm/⅛ inch. Use the cutters to stamp out as many cookies as possible from the dough, cutting each one as close as possible to the next one. Arrange the cookies on the prepared baking sheets. Gather the dough scraps together, knead lightly, re-roll and stamp out more cookies until all the dough has been used up. Bake the gingerbread in batches on the middle shelf of the preheated oven for 10–12 minutes or until firm and lightly browned at the edges. Allow the cookies to cool completely on the baking sheets before decorating.

Prepare the Royal Icing (see page 8). Spoon the icing into a disposable piping bag. Pipe simple clothes and faces onto each cookie and decorate with colourful sugar-coated chocolate drops, stuck on with a small blob of icing. Allow to dry completely before serving.

1 quantity Basic Spiced Gingerbread dough (see page 11)
plain/all-purpose flour, for rolling out

TO DECORATE
½ quantity Royal Icing (see page 8)
assorted sugar-coated chocolate drops

gingerbread-people cutters in assorted sizes
2 prepared baking sheets
a disposable piping bag

MAKES 10–12

375 g/3 cups plain/all-purpose flour

½ teaspoon baking powder

1 teaspoon bicarbonate of/baking soda

3 teaspoons ground ginger

½ teaspoon ground cinnamon

a pinch of cayenne pepper (optional)

a pinch of salt

125 g/1 stick unsalted butter, softened

75 g/⅓ cup dark muscovado sugar

1 egg, lightly beaten

100 ml/⅓ cup golden/corn syrup

TO DECORATE

½ quantity of Royal Icing (see page 8)

edible silver and/or gold balls

shooting star-shaped cookie cutters in assorted sizes

2 prepared baking sheets

a disposable piping bag

MAKES ABOUT 24

SHOOTING STARS

Sift together the flour, baking powder, bicarbonate of/baking soda, ginger, cinnamon, cayenne pepper and salt in a mixing bowl.

Cream the butter and sugar together in the bowl of an electric mixer (or use a large bowl and an electric whisk). Add the beaten egg and golden/corn syrup and mix until smooth. Add the sifted dry ingredients and mix again until smooth.

To knead the dough, first sprinkle a little flour on a clean work surface. Then shape the dough into a ball and push on it and press it onto the work surface, turning it round often. Do this for a minute, then flatten into a disc, cover with clingfilm/plastic wrap and chill for a couple of hours until firm.

Preheat the oven to 180°C (350°F) Gas 4.

Sprinkle more flour on the work surface. Using a rolling pin, roll out the dough to a thickness of about 4 mm/¼ inch. Stamp out shapes with the cookie cutters and arrange on the prepared baking sheets. Gather up any scraps of cookie dough, knead very lightly to bring together into a ball and roll out again to stamp out more cookies. Put the baking sheets on the middle shelf of the preheated oven. Bake for about 10 minutes.

Remove the cookies from the oven and leave to cool on the baking sheets for a couple of minutes before transferring to a wire rack to cool completely.

Spoon the royal icing into a disposable piping bag. Pipe icing onto the cookies as shown and decorate with silver balls. Leave on a wire rack to dry completely before serving.

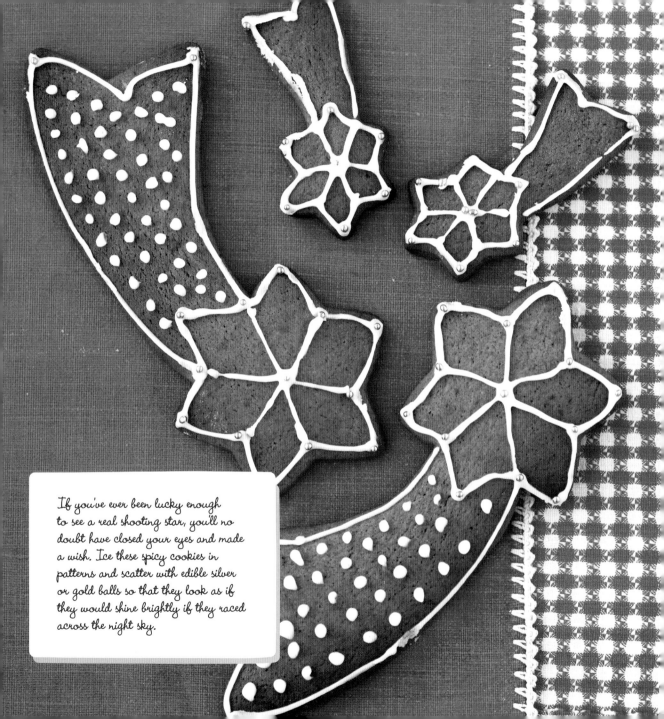

If you've ever been lucky enough to see a real shooting star, you'll no doubt have closed your eyes and made a wish. Ice these spicy cookies in patterns and scatter with edible silver or gold balls so that they look as if they would shine brightly if they raced across the night sky.

EDIBLE GIFTS

These crisp, spiced cookies with a hint of tangy clementine are pretty baked as stars but you can experiment with other shapes – hearts are cute too. Not only do they taste delicious, they also make a perfect gift once threaded with ribbons, boxed and presented as if they were Christmas decorations.

SPICED BROWN SUGAR & CLEMENTINE STARS

100 g/6½ tablespoons butter, softened and cubed

75 g/⅓ cup dark muscovado or dark brown soft sugar

1 teaspoon golden/corn syrup

1 egg, lightly beaten

200 g/1⅔ cups plain/all-purpose flour, sifted

1 teaspoon baking powder

grated zest of 1 clementine

2 teaspoons ground cinnamon

a generous pinch each of ground nutmeg, allspice and cloves

TO DECORATE

100 g/⅔ cup icing/confectioners' sugar

6–7 teaspoons lemon juice

edible silver balls

edible white glitter

star-shaped cookie cutters in assorted sizes

2 prepared baking sheets

MAKES ABOUT 30

Put the butter, sugar and golden/corn syrup in an electric mixer (or use a large mixing bowl and an electric whisk) and mix until combined. Add the beaten egg little by little, alternating with a spoonful of flour, and still mixing. Add the rest of the flour, the baking powder, clementine zest and spices. Mix to combine.

Tip the dough onto a lightly floured work surface and bring it together in a ball. Press the ball into a disc, wrap in clingfilm/plastic wrap and refrigerate for at least 30 minutes.

Preheat the oven to 200°C (400°F) Gas 6.

Halve the chilled dough and roll one half out on the lightly floured work surface until it is about 4 mm/¼ inch thick. Cut out stars with the cookie cutters and arrange the shapes on one of the prepared baking sheets. Gently re-form and re-roll the dough, then keep stamping out stars. Use a cocktail stick/toothpick to make a hole in the top of each cookie.

Repeat with the other half of the dough. Bake in the preheated oven for 8–10 minutes for smaller stars (about 6 cm/2½ inches) and 12–14 minutes for larger stars (about 8.5 cm/3½ inches). When they are ready, the dough will have risen slightly and the edges will be tinged with brown. Transfer to wire racks to cool.

To decorate, sift the icing/confectioners' sugar into a bowl and stir in the lemon juice – add it little by little until you have a drizzling consistency. Decorate each star with a little icing (you can pipe it if you are feeling fancy). Finish with edible silver balls and glitter and thread some fine ribbon through the holes to finish.

COOKIE FAVOURS

200 g/1 stick plus 5 tablespoons unsalted butter

100 g/½ cup caster/granulated sugar

450 g/3 cups plain/all-purpose flour

½ teaspoon baking powder

1 egg

1 teaspoon vanilla extract

TO DECORATE

1 quantity Royal Icing (see page 8)

red, green and yellow food colouring pastes

a selection of coloured writing icing tubes

edible metallic balls

a pack of mini marshmallows

cookies cutters in assorted shapes

2 prepared baking sheets

MAKES ABOUT 24

Preheat the oven to 180°C (350°F) Gas 4.

In a large mixing bowl, mix up the butter, sugar, flour, baking powder, egg and vanilla extract and form into a dough ball. Divide this into four and wrap in cling film/plastic wrap, then refrigerate.

Flour a wooden board and rolling pin and roll out the first piece of dough to a thickness of 3-4 mm/¼ inch. Cut out shapes using the cookie cutters and arrange on the baking sheets. Re-roll the trimmings to cut more shapes. Repeat with the other pieces of dough.

Place the baking sheets in a preheated oven for about 10 minutes until the edges of the shapes are just beginning to turn golden. Allow the cookies to cool on the baking sheets for a few minutes before transferring them to a cooling rack.

Make up the Royal Icing and add sufficient water to create a smooth and runny, icing. Divide this icing into 3 bowls and colour each one with a different food colouring pastes.

Put out the cooled cookies, icing, writing icing tubes, edible balls and mini marshmallows on a table covered with a wipe clean cloth and invite the children to decorate them. Wait until the icing has set completely before packing into cellophane bags and finishing with a ribbon.

Christmas cookies make an enchanting gift. A simple recipe, a set of cookie cutters, some icing tubes and a selection of fun sprinkles is all you need. Package these in cellophane bags and tie with a pretty ribbon ready to lay on the festive table or take a basket of them into school or to the office to hand out to classmates or colleagues instead of Christmas cards.

This decorative and delicious gingerbread house makes a fabulous table centrepiece for Christmas and will elicit oohs and aahs of admiration when it is unveiled! For a traditional look, decorate the gingerbread with white icing, sweets and candy canes, as well as silver sugar balls.

GINGERBREAD HOUSE

Sift the flour, baking powder, bicarbonate/baking of soda, spices and salt together into a mixing bowl and set aside. Put the butter and muscovado sugar in a second bowl and beat until fluffy. Add the egg and golden/corn syrup and mix until smooth. Add the sifted dry ingredients and mix again until smooth.

Flour a clean work surface. Shape the dough into a ball and push on it and press it onto the work surface, turning it round often. Do this for a minute, then flatten into a disc, cover with clingfilm/plastic wrap and chill until firm. Repeat these steps to make a second quantity of gingerbread dough. When you are ready the bake the house, preheat the oven to 180°C (350°F) Gas 4.

To make templates for the house, take a large sheet of paper and draw a rectangle measuring 20 x 11 cm/8 x 4½ inches for the roof. Make another paper rectangle measuring 19 x 10 cm/7½ x 4 inches for the front and back walls. You will also need a template for the sides - this will be a 10-cm/4-inches square with a 4-cm/1½-inch high triangle on top.

Sprinkle more flour on the work surface. Using a rolling pin, roll out the dough to a thickness of about 3-4 mm/¼ inch. Use your paper templates to cut out 2 roof shapes, 2 big walls and 2 sides. Arrange them on the prepared baking sheets.

Bake the gingerbread in batches, for about 10-15 minutes each, until firm and just starting to brown at the edges. Remove from the oven and leave to cool completely.

Make up the Royal Icing and spoon it into the piping bag. Take one gingerbread side and pipe a line of icing along the bottom and up one side. Hold it up on a serving tray or platter. Take a big wall and pipe some icing along the bottom and 2 sides. Hold this at a right angle to the first, iced side. Pick up the second big wall and pipe some icing along the bottom and 2 sides. Hold this in place opposite the other wall and so that it meets the side at a right angle. Repeat with the remaining side. Once the walls are completely set and secure, attach the roof. Pipe a line of icing down the gables and position one roof panel on either side of the gables. Pipe a line of icing across the top of the roof. Hold the roof in place until the icing is firm. To decorate, pipe patterns onto the roof panels. Pipe windows and doors, as well as icicles, and decorate with a sweets/candies as shown here or as you like.

Make up this recipe twice:

375 g/3 cups plain/all-purpose flour

½ teaspoon baking powder

1 teaspoon bicarbonate of/baking soda

3 teaspoons ground ginger

½ teaspoon ground cinnamon

¼ teaspoon each of ground cloves and allspice

a pinch of salt

125 g/1 stick unsalted butter, softened

75 g/⅓ cup dark muscovado sugar

1 egg, lightly beaten

100 ml/⅓ cup golden/corn syrup

TO DECORATE

1 quantity Royal Icing (see page 8)

edible silver balls

assorted sweets/candies

3 prepared baking sheets

a piping bag, fitted with a plain nozzle

SERVES 12

CRUNCHY CHRISTMAS TREES

125 g/1 stick butter
125 g/⅔ cup caster/granulated sugar
1 whole egg
250 g/2 cups plain/all-purpose flour

TO DECORATE
1 egg white, lightly beaten
100 g/¾ cup finely chopped pistachios
icing/confectioners' sugar, for dusting
    (optional)

2 prepared baking sheets
Christmas tree-shaped cookie cutters
    in assorted sizes

MAKES 20-25

Preheat the oven to 180°C (350°F) Gas 4.

Beat the butter and sugar together in a large mixing bowl until smooth. Add the whole egg and beat until fully incorporated. Stir in the flour and bring the mixture together to make a soft, but not sticky dough. Wrap in clingfilm/plastic wrap and chill in the fridge for 30 minutes.

On a clean, lightly floured work surface, roll the dough out into a large rectangle about 3-4 mm/¼ inch. thick. Cut out Christmas trees using the cookie cutters. Lay them on the prepared baking sheets, leaving a little space for spreading between each one. Bring the trimmed dough together and roll out again to cut as many cookies out of the dough as possible. Arrange on the baking sheets with the other cookies.

Brush the top of each cookie with the lightly beaten egg white, leaving the trunk of the tree without the egg white wash. Scatter the chopped pistachios over the branch part of the tree.

Bake in the preheated oven for 10-15 minutes, until golden and firm. Leave to cool on the baking sheets for 5 minutes or so, before transferring to a wire rack to cool completely.

Dust with icing/confectioners' sugar to emulate freshly fallen snow, if liked.

These crunchy, pretty little pistachio-coated trees look really festive at Christmas time and are perfect for packaging up in brown paper and tied with ribbon to give as a grown-up edible gifts to friends and family.

Use an extra-large simple gingerbread man cutter to create these fun giant santa cookies. This recipe makes about six cookies, but if preferred you can use a standard sized cutter to make a bigger batch of these jolly fellows.

SMILING SANTAS

Prepare the Basic Spiced Gingerbread dough according to the recipe on page 11. Preheat the oven to 170°C (325°F) Gas 3.

Lightly dust a clean, dry surface with flour and roll the dough evenly to a thickness of 2–3 mm/⅛ inch. Use the cutters to stamp out 6 large shapes from the dough, cutting each one as close as possible to the next one. Arrange the cookies on the prepared baking sheets. Gather the dough scraps together, knead lightly, re-roll and stamp out more cookies until all the dough has been used up. Bake the gingerbread in batches on the middle shelf of the preheated oven for 10–12 minutes or until firm and lightly browned at the edges. Allow the cookies to cool completely on the baking sheets before icing.

Prepare the Royal Icing. Spoon half of the icing into another bowl and tint it a deep red colour using the food colouring paste (see page 9 for help on Tinting). Fill a disposable piping bag with 3 tablespoons of the white icing and pipe an outline around the suit and hat of each santa and add the fur trims. Finish with a smiley face. Leave to dry for at least 10 minutes. Fill the second piping bag with the red icing and use to flood the cookie to colour in the suit and hat (see page 9 for help with Flooding).

Allow icing to dry for at least 20 minutes before moving, and to dry completely before packaging.

1 quantity Basic Spiced Gingerbread dough (see page 11)

TO DECORATE
1 quantity Royal Icing (see page 8)
red food colouring paste

an extra large (20-cm/8-inch-tall) gingerbread-man cutter
2 prepared baking sheets
2 disposable piping bags

MAKES 6 COOKIES

FLORENTINES

50 g/⅓ cup whole glacé cherries

50 g/⅓ cup mixed candied peel

100 g/⅔ cup sultanas/golden raisins

200 g/1½ cups flaked/slivered almonds

50 g/6 tablespoons plain/all-purpose flour

120 g/1 stick salted butter

160 g/¾ cup caster/granulated sugar

50 ml/3 tablespoons single/light cream

200 g/6½ oz. dark chocolate, roughly chopped

2 prepared baking sheets

5-cm/2-inch round cookie cutter (optional)

MAKES ABOUT 30

Preheat the oven to 170°C (325°F) Gas 3.

Wash all the syrup from the glacé cherries, dry thoroughly and dice finely. If the pieces of mixed peel are large, dice these the same size as the cherries. Place the diced cherries, mixed peel, sultanas/golden raisins, flaked/slivered almonds and flour in a large bowl.

In a saucepan set over low heat, melt the butter and sugar together. Remove from the heat and stir in the cream, then add this to the ingredients in the bowl. Stir until evenly blended. Spoon 6 walnut-size scoops of the mixture onto each baking sheet, spaced well apart, gently pressing down the mounds with the back of the spoon. Bake in the preheated oven for 15 minutes or until golden. Remove from the oven and immediately re-shape the florentines into circles – a cookie cutter is ideal for this, or you can use a knife. Transfer to a wire rack to cool and repeat the process until all the mixture is used and baked.

Melt the chocolate in a heatproof bowl set over a pan of barely simmering water. Do not let the base of the bowl touch the water. Remove from the heat and allow to cool, stirring occasionally, until it has thickened to a spreading consistency. Brush some melted chocolate on the underside of each florentine using a pastry brush and leave to set.

The florentines will keep for 7–10 days in an airtight container or freeze for up to 2 months.

These chewy and delicious Italian bites, full of fruit and nuts with chocolate-coated bases, are great to serve with after-dinner coffee or to crumble over vanilla ice cream. They also make a sophisticated gift.

These sparkly snowflakes are simply made from
a basic meringue so are a useful gluten-free
alternative to a baked cookie and just as welcome!

MERINGUE SNOWFLAKES

Preheat the oven to 200°C (400°F) Gas 6.

Tip the sugar into a small roasting pan. Put it in the preheated oven for about 5 minutes until hot to the touch – be careful not to burn your fingers! Turn the oven down to 110°C (225°F) Gas ¼.

Place the egg whites in a large, clean mixing bowl or in the bowl of an electric mixer. Beat the egg whites (with an electric whisk, if necessary) until they are frothy.

Tip the hot sugar onto the egg whites in one go and continue to whisk on high speed for about 5 minutes until the meringue mixture is very stiff, white and cold.

Spoon the meringue mixture into the prepared piping bag. Pipe little blobs of meringue onto the prepared baking trays in the shape of snowflakes. Scatter silver balls or sprinkle edible glitter over the top. Transfer the baking sheets to the preheated oven.

Bake for about 45 minutes or until the meringues are crisp and dry. Turn off the oven, leave the door closed and let the snowflakes cool down completely inside the oven. They will be fragile so take care when handling and packaging.

150 g/¾ cup caster/granulated sugar
75 g/2½ oz. egg whites (about 2 UK medium/US large egg whites)

TO DECORATE
edible silver glitter and edible silver balls, to decorate

a piping bag, fitted with a star-shaped nozzle
2 prepared baking sheets

MAKES ABOUT 12

TRADITIONS

'Lebkuchen' are traditional German Christmas cookies with a good hint of ginger and spices. They can be covered with either a simple white glacé icing or a coating of dark chocolate glaze.

LEBKUCHEN

2 tablespoons clear honey

2 tablespoons black treacle/molasses

40 g/2½ tablespoons unsalted butter

75 g/⅓ cup dark brown soft sugar

grated zest of ½ orange and ½ lemon

225 g/1¾ cups self-raising/rising flour

½ teaspoon ground cinnamon

2 teaspoons ground ginger

¼ teaspoon grated nutmeg

a pinch of ground cloves

a pinch of salt

50 g/⅓ cup ground almonds

1 egg, lightly beaten

edible silver balls

TO DECORATE

175 g/6 oz. dark chocolate, chopped

1 tablespoon sunflower oil

250 g/2 cups icing/confectioners' sugar

2-3 tablespoons lemon juice

small cookie cutters in assorted shapes
2 prepared baking sheets

MAKES ABOUT 30

Put the honey, treacle/molasses, butter, sugar and orange and lemon zest in a small saucepan. Put it over low heat and stir until the butter has melted and everything is well mixed. Carefully remove from the heat and leave to cool.

Sift the flour, spices and salt together into a mixing bowl, then add the ground almonds. Add the melted butter mixture and the beaten egg and mix until you get a dough.

To knead the dough, sprinkle a little flour on a clean work surface. Shape the dough into a ball and push on it and press it onto the work surface, turning it round often. Do this for just a minute or so until smooth, then wrap in clingfilm/plastic wrap and chill in the fridge for at least 4 hours or overnight.

When you are ready to bake the Lebkuchen, preheat the oven to 180°C (350°F) Gas 4. On the floured work surface, roll the dough out to a thickness of 5 mm/ ¼ inch using a rolling pin. Stamp out shapes with your cookie cutters.

Place the Lebkuchen on the prepared baking sheets and put them in the preheated oven. Bake for about 15-20 minutes, or until just begining to brown at the edges.

Remove the Lebkuchen from the oven and transfer to a wire rack to cool.

To decorate, make a chocolate glaze by melting the chocolate with the oil in a heatproof bowl set over a pan of barely simmering water. Leave to cool for about 10 minutes before using. Prepare a glacé icing by sifting the icing sugar into a bowl and, using a balloon whisk, gradually stir in enough lemon juice to make a smooth mixture that will coat the back of a spoon. Spread chocolate glaze and glacé icing over some of the cooled lebkuchen using a palette knife. Use the tines of a fork dipped into glaze or icing to drizzle contrasting lines onto the cookies. Sprinkle some with edible silver balls to finish. Leave to set completely before serving.

CARDAMOM SHORTBREAD

Preheat the oven to 160°C (325°F) Gas 2.

Put all the ingredients in a large mixing bowl and work until the mixture comes together to form a smooth dough. Shape it into a long sausage shape with a diameter of about 7 cm/3 inches, and wrap in clingfilm/plastic wrap. Refrigerate for about 30 minutes, until firm.

Use a sharp knife to slice the chilled sausage into discs of about 5 mm/¼ inch thick and place on the prepared baking sheet leaving space between each one for the cookies to spread.

Bake in the preheated oven for about 15 minutes, or until firm and golden. Remove from the oven and transfer to a wire rack to cool. Dust dust with caster/superfine sugar and store in an airtight container until ready to enjoy.

120 g/1 stick unsalted butter, softened
160 g/1¼ cups plain/all-purpose flour
60 g/⅓ cup caster/superfine sugar, plus extra for dusting
a pinch of salt
seeds from 5–6 cardamom pods, crushed

1 prepared baking sheet

MAKES 20-24

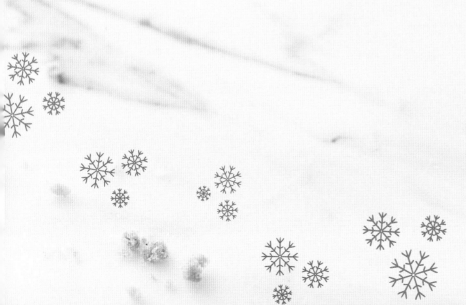

Buttery, melt-in-the-mouth Scottish shortbread is a Christmas tradition and often given as a gift in attractive tins. Why not try something a little different and bake a batch of these cardamom-scented and delicately flavoured shortbread cookies.

These moist chewy cookies (called Ricciarelli in Italian) originated in the beautiful Tuscan town of Siena. Nowadays, they are a favourite all over Italy, and the delightful thing is that they're very easy to make at home.

SOFT ALMOND COOKIES

250 g/8 oz. ready-made marzipan

100 g/½ cup caster/granulated sugar

1 teaspoon Grand Marnier or other orange-flavoured liqueur

1 egg white

150 g/1 cup blanched almonds, finely ground

icing/confectioners' sugar, for dusting

1 prepared baking sheet

MAKES 16–18

Preheat the oven to 180°C (350°F) Gas 4.

Put the marzipan in a blender and process to a paste. Add the caster/granulated sugar and Grand Marnier and process again. Transfer the paste to a bowl and beat in the egg white. Stir in the ground almonds.

Form the mixture into 16–18 small logs about 1.5 cm/½ inch wide and 4 cm/1½ inches long, and lay them out on the prepared baking sheet, with room for spreading between each. Leave to stand in a cool place for 30 minutes, if possible.

Bake the cookies in the preheated oven for 8-10 minutes, until golden. Leave to cool a little on the baking sheet, and then transfer to a wire rack to cool completely. Dust with icing/confectioners' sugar just before serving.

200 g/1½ cups plain/all-purpose flour

1½ teaspoons baking powder

100 g/½ cup golden/unrefined
caster/granulated sugar

30 g/¼ cup pistachio kernels

30 g/¼ cup hazelnuts

30 g/¼ cup sultanas/golden raisins

4 dried apricots, quartered

4 dried figs, quartered

freshly grated zest of 1 small lemon

2 eggs, lightly beaten

1 prepared baking sheet

MAKES ABOUT 28

FIG, APRICOT & NUT BISCOTTI

Preheat the oven to 150°C (300°F) Gas 2.

Sift the flour and baking powder into a mixing bowl. Stir in the sugar, pistachio nuts, hazelnuts, sultanas, apricots, figs and lemon zest.

Pour in the eggs and mix well until you get a dough-like mixture. Bring the dough together into a ball in your hands and transfer it to the prepared baking sheet.

Flour your hands and roll the dough into a log (you can use the greaseproof paper to help you roll the dough). Flatten it so that it is about 8 cm/3 inches wide.

Bake in the preheated oven for about 30 minutes. To check if it's ready, press very lightly on top of the log and if it springs back you can take it out of the oven. If it still feels very firm, leave it in the oven for a few more minutes. When it is ready, remove from the oven and leave to cool for about 10 minutes.

Using a large, serrated bread knife, slice the log into 5-mm/¼-inch slices. Lay the slices on the baking sheet and return to the hot oven for 10 minutes, turning them halfway through cooking. When they are pale gold, remove from the oven and leave to cool for a few minutes before serving. Store in an airtight container for up to 2 weeks.

These double-baked crisp cookies are packed with dried fruit and nuts, and are made lighter without butter. They are best enjoyed with a cup of strong coffee or dipped in some vanilla ice cream for a sweet dessert treat.

These crumbly, vanilla-scented biscuits really do have to be piped into elegant shapes for full effect. The underside of each cookie is coated in chocolate but you could just as easily dip the ends of each one into melted chocolate if you prefer. For a festive feel you could use red, white and green Christmas sprinkles or white glitter sprinkles for a pretty snowdusted effect.

VIENNESE FINGERS

Preheat the oven to 170°C (325°F) Gas 3.

Cream the butter, sugar and vanilla extract with an electric whisk or stand mixer until pale and light – about 2 minutes. Sift the flour, cornflour/cornstarch, baking powder and salt into the bowl and gently mix again until smooth and thoroughly combined.

Spoon the dough into the piping bag and pipe tight S-shaped spirals onto the prepared baking sheet. Bake on the middle shelf of the preheated oven for 10-12 minutes or until pale golden.

Remove the cookies from the oven and allow to cool on the baking sheet for about 5 minutes, then carefully transfer to a wire rack using a palette knife or fish slice and allow to cool completely.

Melt both chocolates together in a heatproof bowl set over a pan of barely simmering water. Do not let the base of the bowl touch the water. Remove from the heat, stir until smooth and allow to cool slightly.

Dip the underside of each cooled cookie into the melted chocolate, scatter your chosen sprinkles over the chocolate-coated edges and allow to set on baking parchment before serving.

125 g/1 stick butter, soft

40 g/⅓ cup icing/confectioners' sugar

1 teaspoon pure vanilla extract

125 g/1 cup plain/all-purpose flour

2 tablespoons cornflour/cornstarch

¼ teaspoon baking powder

a pinch of salt

TO DECORATE
50 g/1¾ oz. each dark and milk/semisweet chocolate, chopped (or all white chocolate if you prefer)

sprinkles of your choice

a piping bag fitted with a large star-shaped nozzle/tip

1 prepared baking sheet

MAKES ABOUT 15

COCONUT SNOWBALLS

100 g/6½ tablespoons butter, softened

150 g/¾ cup caster/granulated sugar

1 egg

200 g/1⅔ cups plain/all-purpose flour

1 generous teaspoon baking powder

finely grated zest of 1 orange

TO DECORATE

100 g/scant ½ cup seedless orange marmalade

150 g/1⅓ cups desiccated/shredded coconut

2 prepared baking sheets

MAKES 25-30

Preheat the oven to 180°C (350°F) Gas 4.

Beat the butter and sugar together in a large mixing bowl until smooth. Add the egg, and continue to beat until fully incorporated. Stir in the flour, baking powder and orange zest and bring the mixture together to form a stiff dough.

Roll the mixture into small balls the size of walnuts and lay on the prepared baking sheets, leaving a little space for spreading between each one. Pat down lightly for a flat finish (as pictured) or leave ball-shaped for a snowball bite.

Bake in the preheated oven for about 10 minutes, until light golden and firm.

Leave on the baking sheet for 5 minutes or so to cool slightly, and then transfer to a wire rack to cool completely.

Put the dessicated/shredded coconut in a wide, shallow dish and set aside.

When the snowballs are cold, gently warm the marmalade in a small saucepan set over a low heat and brush it over the entire surface of the snowballs. Press or roll the cookies in the coconut to coat and leave to set.

Store in an airtight container or cookie jar and eat within 1 week.

These look so pretty. Fans of coconut will adore them.
If preferred, you can coat the finished cookies in white
chocolate rather than marmalade for an even more
effective snowball appearance that kids will love!

Marzipan is one of life's little luxuries and a traditional indulgence at Christmastime. It gives these mini cookies a heady almond flavour and makes them delicately chewy. Flavoured with cinnamon and spices, these stars are delicious served with warm mulled wine for a festive and warming treat.

MARZIPAN STARS

Preheat the oven to 180°C (350°F) Gas 4.

Break the marzipan into small pieces and put these in a bowl with the butter. Cream together until the mixture is paste-like. Sift in the flour and add the ground almonds, almond meal, vanilla extract and spices and beat to a smooth, soft dough. The mixture should be very soft but not sticky so add a little more flour if needed.

Dust a work surface with flour. Roll out the dough to a 1-cm/½-inch thickness using a rolling pin. Use the cutter to stamp out 35 stars. Arrange the stars on the baking sheets a small distance apart as they will spread a little during baking. Bake in the preheated oven for 10–15 minutes, until golden brown. Remove from the oven and leave to cool slightly on the baking sheet.

To ice, whisk the egg white to stiff peaks and sift in the powdered fondant icing sugar. Fold together until you have a smooth icing. Use a pastry brush to coat the tops of the cookies whilst they are still warm. Leave to set for 5 minutes then apply a second coat of icing. Allow the icing to set completely before serving.

These cookies will keep for up to 2 weeks if stored in an airtight container.

200 g/⅔ cup marzipan

90 g/6 tablespoons unsalted butter, softened

60 g/scant ½ cup self-raising/rising flour

120 g/1¼ cups ground almonds

30 g/2 tablespoons almond meal

1 teaspoon vanilla extract

1 teaspoon ground cinnamon

1 teaspoon mixed spice/apple pie spice

TO DECORATE

1 egg white (see note on page 4)

100 g/¾ cup powdered fondant icing sugar

a 5-cm/2-inch star-shaped cookie cutter

2 prepared baking sheets

MAKES ABOUT 35

CHESTNUT-CHOC-CHIP COOKIES

100 g/7 tablespoons butter, at room temperature and chopped

80 g/7 tablespoons caster/granulated sugar

35 g/3 tablespoons muscovado or soft brown sugar

1 teaspoon pure vanilla extract

1 teaspoon single/light cream

1 egg

100 g/¾ cup plain/all-purpose flour

60 g/scant ½ cup chestnut flour

½ teaspoon baking powder

¼ teaspoon salt

85 g/½ cup milk chocolate chips

55 g/⅓ cup cocoa nibs

50 g/2 oz. candied chestnuts, chopped

1-2 prepared baking sheets

MAKES ABOUT 25

Put the butter in a bowl and beat with a wooden spoon until very soft. Beat in the sugars until well incorporated and creamy, then add the vanilla extract, cream and egg and beat in. Gradually sift in the flours, baking powder and salt and mix until combined. Finally, mix in the chocolate chips, cocoa nibs and candied chestnuts until evenly distributed.

Cover and refrigerate the dough for 30 minutes.

Preheat the oven to 170°C (325°F) Gas 3.

Remove the bowl from the fridge. Lightly flour a clean work surface and roll the chilled dough out into a sausage roughly 30 cm/12 inches long. Cut the dough into about 25 equal slices and arrange on the prepared baking sheets.

Bake in the preheated oven for about 15-20 minutes until golden brown. Allow the cookies to cool on the baking sheets for 5 minutes, then transfer to a wire rack to finish cooling.

This is the ultimate Christmas cookie luxury for the true gourmet! It is a treasure trove of decadent flavours, baked with chestnut flour and studded with cocoa nibs and candied chestnuts. Share a batch of these with family and friends if you can, or selfishly on your own if you can't...

INDEX